STEPS TO A SUCCESSFUL APARTMENT GARDEN

TABLE OF CONTENTS

INTRODUCTION

With spring arriving all over the country many people are considering starting a garden. If you live in an apartment, you might be lamenting the fact you have no yard or space for the relaxing and enjoyable process of growing your own food. However, it takes less space than you think to grow plants and even a small apartment can benefit from the advantages of a few vegetables or fruit pots.

Of course, since space is at a premium in an apartment it can be difficult to know where to put your garden. A balcony or small patio is of course the obvious choice if you have them, but even apartments without an outdoor area can successfully grow a few plants. Just look for "shade-loving" varieties of fruits, vegetables, and flowers for best indoor results. If you can find a windowsill that gets a good amount of sunlight you have a perfect location for a small garden in various containers.

Of course, since your garden will be a container garden as opposed to a standard plot of ground, you can incorporate more decorative items or theme into your pots to make them more attractive. For example, all kinds of bottles, recycled containers, baskets, and boxes make a perfect place to put a plant. A "green" theme could use empty milk cartons, cereal boxes, and other recycled materials to hold a variety of plants. Or you could choose a color and make all your containers match that color: blue glass bottles, blue baskets, blue pots, etc. Even containers you might not think of at first like a football helmet or cowboy boot can be a plant holder if you are creative.

The biggest caution experts give for a new gardener is to take it slow. Plants do require care, so don't plant more than you can easily handle. Even a couple of plants can brighten an apartment so consider choosing only your favorite two or three fruits, vegetables, or flowers to cultivate this year and see how it goes. Remember that most plants need well-drained soil so consider using a small pot inside of a larger one in order to allow water a chance to drain out of the plant without making a mess in your apartment. If you don't have a lot of time to devote to caring for a garden, consider growing cactus or a water garden that doesn't need much attention. Anyone can have a garden, even in a small apartment. All it takes is a little more creativity and imagination for a beautiful spot of green heaven in your apartment.

CHAPTER 1
APARTMENT GARDENING

This residential apartment is located on landscaped property that is at ground level. This term loosely describes any apartment on the first floor. It also includes a basement apartment or one in a high rise. If it is a real garden apartment, there will be no household, or apartment, above it. They are spread out horizontally in an open courtyard. You can find these apartments worldwide.

Such an apartment will have one or two bedrooms but you can find some that have three or more bedrooms, especially if they are used as a vacation apartment. The more bedrooms there are the more people they can accommodate when on vacation and renting the apartment. If it is an apartment that is rented out long term it is generally not furnished. If the apartment is rented out on a weekly or monthly basis for vacations, it will be furnished. Garden apartments may also have one or two stories. The common area can include outdoor amenities like a swimming pool, tennis or basketball courts, a spa or clubhouse. The entrance to the apartment could be off the courtyard or the street.

The owners of the garden apartments are responsible for the outdoor area being kept up with the lawn mowed, any outdoor equipment cleaned, clean swimming pool without leaves and other debris, etc. Many owners will plant the area with well cared for trees and floors. If it is an apartment complex and you have a pet you need to find out if there is a special area for the dogs. Make sure that you clean up after your dog once it has finished its business. Your garden apartment may have a small yard or patio. If your garden apartment has either of these two amenities, it would be a good place to have friends and family over for a barbeque.

Each garden apartment is a separate household unit but all of the tenants share any amenities, such as a swimming pool or exercise room and the main outside grounds. The apartments have their own controls for the heat and air conditioning and bathroom and kitchen facilities. In some places, it may be called a walk-up garden apartment because it has an outdoor staircase. With garden apartment complexes that offer premium services like a weight and exercise room or sauna may be charged an extra monthly fee to help with the upkeep and have a key to let them into these facilities. By having a key, it prevents those that choose not to pay the extra fee from using these premium facilities. Some may even have a laundry room for the residents. The rent for a garden apartment would be much the same as a regular apartment but it depends on the location and amenities.

GARDEN IDEAS FOR YOUR APARTMENT

Living in a group of rooms a few floors high inside a concrete building need not be constricting and stressful. With a little guidance and abundant creativity, even the smallest cramped spaces can be turned into the haven each home ought to be. The same goes for apartment homeowners who have dreamt of their own backyards when they were kids. Here are some directional tips and landscape supply options to create that sky-high garden you've always wanted.

Stretch your garden beyond the balcony. When browsing the local landscape supply store, instead of limiting yourself to items that would fit inside your balcony, select structures that would fit inside your apartment. This goes for condo units that do not have balconies at all. With enough fresh air and sunlight entering the room, whether from a window or skylight, certain plants can be sustained indoors.

Look up. A traditional garden is on the ground, for obvious reasons. Apartment gardens, in order to contain various flora, should have small plants that are displayed vertically on a wall or stacked in shelves. Keep an eye out for landscape supplies that can be hung or are taller than they are wider. You can even use an old skid or dresser to store your plants.

Match what's to the left and right of your garden. Select a landscape theme that would complement the rest of the condominium. Whether you make it the highlight or not, the garden should harmonize with everything else in your home and agree with your central theme. Coordinate colors, shapes, sizes and textures.

Make it go a long way. Creeping and crawling vines make for a good backdrop against a vintage table and chair set. Check out your local landscape supply shop for trellises and cyclone wires that could fit your needs. Remember that these vines require a lot of maintenance before and even after you've reached the desired wall of leaves.

"SEN" it down. While you want the garden bright and lively, avoid cramming in too many things into that tiny space. Organize your landscape theme into patterns or sizes. Color-code them to make it more aesthetically pleasing. Use the Zen gardening principles of keeping things Serene, Enjoyable and

Natural.

An apartment may have a lot of limitations in terms of what you can and cannot do and this can even make picking out a good theme, a daunting task. Take all these limitations in stride, think of them as a challenge to your imagination and determination.

CHAPTER 2
STARTING AN APARTMENT GARDEN

Ask any apartment fan with thumbs even the lightest shade of green, and they'll tell you that an at-home garden is one of life's little treasures to be sure. But for the uninitiated, diving in to the world of plant life can be a daunting task. So how best to start your own apartment garden?

Your first course of action should be to determine the size and scope of your new undertaking, based, fittingly, on the size of your apartment layout. If you are fortunate enough to have a patio of some sort, get ready to celebrate! These garden domiciles are perfect for growing traditional veggies as well as more advanced climbers such as tomatoes (don't forget that hanging pole!). If you are lacking an outdoor area, fear not; consider putting a reasonably-sized table under the most available source of natural window light.

Be aware of your surroundings and take that into account in regards to what you want to plant. If you live in Arizona or Alaska, odds are good you'll be a tad more limited in your selection than, say, sunny California. Even in the most desirable of climates most plants still have a season-based cycle, so be sure to read up as much as you can on the veggies you aim to grow. Annuals are always a good choice, minimizing your investment and maximizing your return, but again be sure to take things like temperature and sunlight amounts into account.

If space is a major concern, consider scaling down your garden to primarily focus upon herbs. It's still a great way to add freshness to your apartment cooking, while containing your garden to a smaller aquarium or pot. Containers such as 20 gallon Rubbermaid tub can be great makeshift gardens, just be sure to drill holes in the bottom before filling them with dirt. It is also probably a good idea to scope out what lies below, so you don't accidentally drench your neighbor's head. Speaking of safety concerns, if you have small children be sure to plant only non-toxic plants (and avoid those cacti while you're at it).

Remember, planting a garden around your apartment can be a great joy, and there's nothing quite like feasting on produce you've tended with your own hands. Just be sure to keep on top of your new hobby to prevent your patio from evolving into a habitat from 'Where The Wild Things Are'!

HOW TO START AN APARTMENT GARDEN - 5 STEPS TO A SUCCESSFUL APARTMENT GARDEN

When first starting an apartment garden, there are several factors you must take into consideration.

1) Do not pick well shaded areas - This should be done for obvious reasons. As any gardener should know, plants need plenty of sunlight in order to grow to their maximum potential. Without the proper sunlight, the photosynthesis process will not happen.

2) Do your research on what type of seeds to plant - You need to know which type of plants will grow successfully in your climate zone and which ones will not. Most vegetables have different growth rates, depending on the time you have for your garden, you should definitely plan which seeds to plant.

3) Examine the soil content-If you plan on potted plants in your apartment, then buy the proper potting soil. When growing plants outside of your apartment, examine the soil to see if it is suitable for proper plant growth. If not, then just buy the necessary potting soil and do the necessary work to replace the old soil with the new. Of course, check the apartment rules first, about planting outside of your apartment.

4) The proper planting procedures-Before starting the planting process the proper planting supplies need to be obtained. These include, but are not limited to, seeds, shovel, bucket, and fertilizer. The soil is the single most important aspect to a successful apartment garden. Remove all debris throughout the area to be soiled. This can be done with a rake.

5) Add the appropriate amount of fertilizer to the soil- Be careful not to overfertilize the soil. Next dig the trenches, if planting outside. Do not make the columns too close to each other. Plant the seeds according to your measurements and cover them with dirt softly. Before you know you'll be on your way to a successful apartment garden.

THE PERFECT GARDEN STARTS WITH CHOOSING THE RIGHT PLANTS AND FLOWERS

Deciding to plant a garden is something many homeowners and apartment dwellers choose to do and in many cases a garden does not have to be one planted in the ground, it can be a potted garden.

One the decision is made then a visit to the garden center is on the list, this is where all the plants and flowers can be found, bushes and trees and where a professional can help guide the choices made. Not every plant is right for every garden, some need more sunlight than others and some flowers bloom at different times.

The key to a good garden is to have flowers that bloom at different times, plants and foliage that will grow properly in the pots or area the garden will be located with the right amount of sun. The sun can be a deciding factor if a plant or flower will grow properly, too much sun can burn some plants and flowers and to little sun can make some flowers and plants not grow quickly or flower at all.

These are some of the things to be concerned with when planting a garden and by using a garden center the plants will be in perfect shape, they will not be root bound, which is something found when purchasing plants and flowers at other places. The person working at the garden center will be a professional that will be able to answer questions about the plants and flowers helping to make educated decisions on what will work in this garden.

Most gardeners have ideas about what their garden should look like, what type of plants and flowers they want and how they will make it a place of beauty in their yard and this is where visiting the garden center comes in and this is where all the different varieties will be found.

Each plant that is chosen should have a place to be planted that will afford it the amount of light and shade that it will need to have a breathtaking garden, it is this reason that every beautiful flower should not be chosen. Only those that will grow to its full beauty in the location of the garden, this will ensure that the garden will look its best. This again is where the garden center is a place to purchase plants, this is because they will be healthy and clearly marked what type of light and water they will need and if they will grow good in pots for the apartment garden.

Planting a garden can be a thing of joy and it can be a breathtaking site in a yard or on an apartment patio when the right plants and flowers are chosen and the right vegetables to lend their colors. They will also lend special tastes to the table when they have ripened as an extra treat of having a garden and it all begins with the garden center.

CREATE A SCENTED FLOWER GARDEN WITH THESE SIX PLANTS

There are many plants to choose from when creating a garden that delights the nose as well as the eyes. Here are six favorites you can plant together to make a "sense-sational" garden.

Nemesia. This plant creates a profusion of blossoms all summer long. It may fade during extremely hot weather, so let it have a little shade during July and August if you can. Grows on tall, strong stems with small leaves, making the plant look compact and neat. Flower colors include yellow, white, orange, pink, and blue. Likes rich soil and plenty of water. Tolerates partial shade. Pinch the tips of starter plants to promote branching. When flowers start to fade, shake the plants gently to deadhead.

Height: 12-24 inches. Spacing: Plant in groups of three or five, spacing plants 8 inches apart and groups 24 or more inches apart.

Bacopa. This neat plant has small, sage-colored leaves and a profusion of tiny flowers. Grows upright and stays small; ideal ground cover. Fertilize every other week for best growth. Grows best in almost boggy conditions, so don't let the soil dry out.

Flowers in shades of pink and red, purple, and white. Likes partial shade, but will tolerate full morning sun in a location that doesn't get too hot. If planted in a container, try bringing it in next fall and keeping it over the winter. Pinch when you transplant to promote bushiness.

Height: up to 12 inches. Spacing: Plant in containers or in groups of three or five in the garden, spaced 6 inches apart. Space groups 24 inches apart.

Trailing snapdragons. These plants have fine stems and small leaves, giving them an airy appearance. The trumpet-shaped flowers are just sweet to look at as well as to smell. Comes in a variety of colors, including yellow, purple, blue, and orange. Fertilize every two weeks. Likes plenty of moisture and rich soil. Full sun, but will tolerate partial shade. You may pinch off branch tips upon transplanting, but it's not necessary. Pinching later in the season (after bloom) encourages late-season flowering.

Height: Mounded plants reach 8 inches in height. Trails up to 2 feet. Spacing: Plant in containers or in the garden where they can trail without interfering with other flowers.

Nicotiana. This fragrant plant is particularly easy to grow. Flowers open in the late afternoon. Comes in red, white, pink, yellow, and blue shades. Slender stems have fewer leaves than nemesia or bacopa, making them seem very spacious. Plant in groups of five to seven plants for best effect. Attracts hummingbirds. Susceptible to frost, so transplant after all danger of frost is passed. Likes moist soil but not soggy. Fertilize every 2 to 4 weeks throughout the summer. Pinch upon transplanting to promote bushiness. The leaves are somewhat sticky, so be careful when weeding. Deadhead spent flowers to promote rebloom.

Height: 12-36 inches tall, depending on variety. Space: Plant in masses of five to seven plants for best effect, spacing each plant 8-12 inches apart and groups 24 inches apart.

Sweet alyssum. Not only do these plants smell wonderful, they provide a little textural variety to the flower garden with their masses of white blooms and tiny leaves. Does well alongside nemesia and bacopa in partial sun. Fertilize every 2 to 4 weeks. Tolerate dry conditions, but don't mind full moisture. Will grow well in poorer or average soils. A great all-around plant.

Height: 6 to 8 inches. Spacing: Plant along the entire edge of the flower garden, spacing each plant 8 inches apart.

Sweet pea. Cut the flowers when in full bloom and bring them in the house for a delightful, long-lasting bouquet. Cut the whole flower stem to promote rebloom. Pinch transplants when they have four or more pairs of leaves. Do not like hot, dry winds and the heat of high summer. Provide partial shade. Keep moist at all times but not soggy. Likes rich soil, so amend with compost or peat and fertilize every 2 weeks during the growing season.

Height: These are climbers, so provide a trellis for best growth. Be gentle, and add support if necessary. Spacing: 6 inches apart.

Herbs such as lemon balm, rosemary and chocolate mint add a delightful layer to the scented garden, and since it's the leaves that smell pretty, you don't have to wait for your annual flowers to open. Plus, you can add these herbs to your cooking, completing the circle of enjoyment.

Shrubs add yet another lovely layer to the sweet-smelling flower garden, with Honeysuckle, Lilac and Roses being the most popular. You can keep your garden simple by choosing from the sweet annuals and herbs, however, and have a garden you can enjoy with all your senses.

GLITZ UP YOUR GARDEN WITH THESE ACCESSORY PLANTS

Whether your flower garden is 50 feet long or in a five gallon bucket, you can transform a pleasing arrangement into something truly spectacular with "accessory" plants. These babies stay low growing and add sweet scents and masses of color. Hey, you wouldn't put on an evening gown and leave your diamond rings at home, right?

Portulaca (also known as Moss Rose). Moss roses have thick, succulent stems covered with needle-like leaves. Flowers are huge (1 inch or more in diameter) and brightly colored in oranges, reds and neon pink. You can also find pastel flowers, too, so read the tags carefully. These plants love heat and dry conditions and even thrive in sandy soils. If you've got good conditions in your garden, they'll adapt to that, too. Love full sun! Do not fertilize except when you transplant. No need to deadhead, but if plants get scraggly, cut them back and they will recover and re-bloom. The flowers close up on cloudy days and in the evening, so don't be dismayed if your newly transplanted moss roses close their faces right away. Work wonderfully in containers, rock gardens, crevices, and as groundcover. Love to live near strawberries.

Height: 4-8 inches high. Spacing: Moss Roses spread 6-18 inches (usually more around 10 inches). Plant close together at the edge of the container or garden bed.

Ageratum, also known as Floss Flower. These fuzzy lavender or white sweetheart plants create a mass of color in small spaces.

Grows well in containers or in the garden; likes well-drained soil. Will tolerate partial shade but prefers full sun. Bloom non-stop from spring until first frost. Deadhead if the plants start to look untidy and they will re-bloom within a week or so. Great for borders because of the unusual lavender-blue color and masses of flowers.

Height: Mounded plants seldom grow over 10 inches tall. Spacing: Space plants six inches apart for masses of color; great in containers.

Alyssum, sometimes called Sweet Alyssum. The heavenly fragrance of the lacy white flowers makes these a great addition to containers set right by high traffic areas. Will tolerate light shade; please do not overheat or they will wilt and the flowers will fade and fall. Well-drained soil (perfect container plants or at the edges of garden beds). Bloom all summer long; shear off when the majority of flowers have faded and they will recover in a few days.

Height: less than 10 inches. Spacing: Group 3 or 5 plants together 6 inches apart for masses of bloom and fragrance.

Lobelia. This lacy annual comes in a wide variety of spectacular colors. Plant a hanging basket of lobelia for massive, fragrant effect. Lobelia has been a garden favorite for more than 200 years. Likes full sun and rich, moist soil. Does not like heat, so please watch the temperature on your deck. Deadhead by shaking the stems. If the plant goes crazy, you may shear it off and it will recover and re-bloom.

Height: Rarely grows higher than 6 inches, though some stems may stand up. Trailing varieties can reach up to five feet long under the right conditions. Spacing: Place in hanging baskets, window boxes, or tall containers around the edges. Space plants

6 inches apart.

Verbena. This hanging basket essential is just like a family friend. Low-fuss plants come in a huge variety of bloom colors and the lacy leaves look just wonderful in containers and baskets. Please do not pamper your verbena! They don't like a lot of water or fertilizer and will do better with reasonable neglect. Loves full sun all day long. You must deadhead verbena by shearing off 1/4 of the stems. Will re-bloom in a few days, so please be patient. Shear again for continued bloom all summer. If your plant is attacked by spider mites, thrips, or powdery mildew, move it to a sunny spot, shear if off, and spray with insect control spray. (Ask your Beier's associate for recommended insect controllers.) Plants may over winter, so bring them in before first frost and hang in a sunny window.

Height: Rarely grows over 6 inches high but will trail for several feet in a hanging basket or as a ground cover. Spacing: Transplant 6 inches apart in baskets and containers; 12-24 inches apart if using for ground cover.

Dusty Miller. Hey, don't knock a little silver and green foliage plant! It may not produce massive blooms, but this plant is steady and looks great with showier cousins. In fact, cut off the flowers to encourage more silver foliage. Water regularly until plants are established, then allow to dry out between soakings. Too much water will rot Dusty Miller. This plant appreciates a little bone meal, well-rotted manure or compost when they are first transplanted. Bonus: Dusty Miller is deer resistant!

CHAPTER 3

BALCONY GARDENING - JUST BECAUSE YOU DON'T HAVE A PLOT OF LAND DOESN'T MEAN YOU CAN'T GROW A GARDEN

Some gardeners are blessed with an abundance of deep, fertile soil. Some have soil that needs attention before it will grow anything. Others have no soil at all. Those who have none can turn to balcony gardening, a popular activity of those who live in apartments and condominiums. A balcony garden has its limitations, but it is better than none.

Plants in containers, whether they be vegetables on the balcony or house plants in hanging baskets, are in constant danger of stress. Unlike plants in the ground, those in containers have a severely restricted root area with a limited supply of water. Missing only one watering can prove disastrous.

Shallow containers are the worst because they not only dry out quickly but drain poorly. Large barrels or boxes are ideal as long as they don't have to be moved.

Many hanging baskets are too small for outdoor growing because the plants soon fill them with roots, leaving little space for water. With a little ingenuity it should be possible to devise better containers. Wood offers the greatest versatility. When stained, the planters have a natural look. You can also use pressure- treated wood; no staining is necessary.

Deep, round, plastic dishpans are easy to use and, if suspended with strong nylon twine, make excellent hanging pots for balcony gardening. Plastic pails and garbage cans are excellent for both flowers and vegetables. But don't forget the drain holes.

To reduce the watering chore, some kind of wick and reservoir system can be established. Plastic chips which are used for packing fragile objects can be placed in the bottom to form a well. They are then covered with a piece of synthetic fabric and the potting mix is placed on top. The fabric wick will carry water from the well to the mix for a long period. A section of garden hose placed vertically inside the pot will allow you to use a dipstick to measure the depth of water in the well.

Pay close attention to the potting mix, making sure that it is rich in organic matter to hold water and has some porous material to provide aeration. Peat is the safest type of organic matter and perlite or vermiculite is a good aerator because of its light weight. Sand is not a good choice, mainly because it is heavy.

Because frequent watering leaches out nutrients, fertilizer must be added regularly. A soluble fertilizer works well but, even safer and surer, is the slow-release fertilizer sold in many garden stores. It ensures a constant supply without burning the roots.

Balcony gardening is a great alternative for those not lucky enough to have land to plant a garden on. With the right containers, soil and watering you can grow a garden that even the most seasoned garden owners would be proud of.

CONTAINER GARDENING INDOORS AND OUTDOORS

For years people have been gardening in containers, mostly because they lacked space. For some it was because they lived in climates that wouldn't allow them to grow year round. Container gardens afford you the option of planting outside until the cold forces the container inside, next to a sunny window.

Most container gardens were planted by people that lived in apartments but still wanted the addition of color and the feeling of accomplishment when seeing their plants grow. Big, beautiful showy flowers have a tranquil effect that soothes you at the end of a long day. Container gardening need not be limited to apartment gardening, everyone should have their own. Most certainly you don't have to stick to flowers in containers. You can grow vegetables and herbs in pots.

By adding garden pots it allows you to put spots of color around green shrubs or trees to brighten any corner of your yard. Placing containers filled with your favorite flower adds loads of appeal to a walkway or paved patio. The fun part of that is you can rotate the pots to different locations adding a new looks or colors with every move. Putting autumnal colored Mums in pots or spring tulips in a container allows you to landscape by season keeping your garden bright and interesting.

Your container can become a mini garden. For example when we lived in Pennsylvania our front yard screened us from the road with 10 feet tall evergreens. Although it was good for privacy, it made it very hard for guests to find our house. To fix this problem I purchased a half of a whisky barrel painted our name and street number on it and placed on the lawn at the end of the driveway. Then I filled it with some organic matter, planted bright red geraniums in the center and placed trailing ivy along the outer edges. Not only did it help our friends find us but the whole neighborhood used it when giving directions to their friends and family. Everyone would come up to us and say,

"Never move that pot of flowers, it's our favorite landmark."

Don't limit yourself to a barrel, anything can be used, a watering can, an urn or big boldly colored ceramic pots, even a wheelbarrow. Use your imagination when it comes to the containers you will plant. A friend of mine would go to the Italian restaurants around town and ask them for their used large olive oil cans. She'd take them home and plant a bunch of mini gardens. This created an interesting and colorful spot unlike any in the neighborhood. She would plant herbs in some of them so this little garden had two uses.

For container gardening use a fast draining potting soil mixed with a little coarse sand. I always use pots with holes in the bottom to ensure good drainage. You may know exactly how much to water the plant but if you have a rainy spell it could be the demise of the mini garden that has no drainage system. Fertilize well and often, nutrients in a container can leech out.

Repotting will be necessary as the plants will become root bound as they thrive. Just go to the next size container and plant a new flower or herb in the original pot.

Go to your garden nursery center and look through the selections. Choose plants that will harmonize and colors that go well together. Container Gardening is fun and easy and a great way to show off your handiwork.

ORGANIC CONTAINER GARDENING AND HERBS

Organic container gardening can be done even in the smallest apartment. Gardening in this way gives you a fresh supply of herbs that are chemical-free as well as decorating your apartment or patio.

You can control your herbs environment by moving the pots into the sun or shade whenever needed, giving you the chance to create perfect conditions for growing herbs even in poor climates.

Another advantage of organic container gardening is that you can give the herbs just the right soil and nutrients to thrive and do not have to depend on garden soil for a great harvest.

POTTING MIX

Herbs do well in potting soil because it is free of insects and diseases that might be found in the regular garden soil. Garden outlets and landscape places sell organic mix, or you can mix your own soil. Just blend equal parts of:

- natural compost like dry cow or horse manure
- purchased organic potting soil
- washed coarse builders sand.

CONTAINERS

Next, in establishing your organic container gardening is to clean the pots with soapy water and rinse them out well as this minimizes any chance the pots become contaminated. Then line the bottom of the containers with pottery shards or small rocks and fill them 2/3 full with the soil. Allow some space for inserting the plants, then finish filling the pot with soil and remember to leave two inches of space under the rim of the pot for watering the herbs.

PESTS AND INSECTS

One of the advantages of organic container gardening is that it attracts fewer insects than herbs grown in a conventional

21

garden. If you do get insects however, spray them with some soapy water or some leftover black tea.

FAVORITE HERBS

Organic container gardening is easy and gives great results provided that the basic requirements are met. Some ideal herbs for organic container gardening are mint,oregano, sage, thyme, marjoram and basil, which grow well in pots.

INVASIVE HERBS

Be careful not to grow the more invasive herbs together with slow growing herbs like sage. Mint is an example of an herb that should be grown in its own pot because it does eventually take over the space thus preventing the other plant to develop fully.

Organic container gardening takes only a little effort and in return it will beautify your home, provide a wonderful aroma and fresh healthy herbs to enjoy.

ORGANIC INDOOR GARDENING - NOT AS HARD AS IT SOUNDS

Organic gardening sounds intimidating to a lot of people. After all, to qualify for the organic standard, foods from organic farms have to meet some pretty tough criteria. However, it's not really hard to get started on your own organic indoor garden. What's difficult to do on a large scale is simple inside your own home. While you won't be able to grow a lot, you'll have the satisfaction of having your own delicious herbs and small vegetables. You'll also know that they're good for you, because you have control over every aspect of the growing process.

The first step in starting your organic indoor gardening process is deciding what to grow. This will be limited by the amount of space you have, and your conditions. Ideally, apartment gardeners would like to have a flat space, such as a balcony or the rooftop available. However, if you're limited to gardening indoors, you can still succeed. You'll probably have to stick to smaller plants, unless you have a large sunny space that you can dedicate to your organic indoor gardening. Pay attention to the amount of sun your prospective garden space gets throughout the day, and the humidity and other conditions in your home or apartment. Different plants need different amounts of light each day. If you can't provide several hours of full sun, plants such as cherry tomatoes or small peppers won't grow well. You can still grow the type that prefer shade, however.

Herbs are a popular organic indoor garden starter, and make great windowsill plants. You can get them started right in the kitchen, if there's enough sun and a way to protect them from damage. Imagine having your own fresh spice rack, in the form of an organic indoor garden right next to your cooking area. Choose from popular herbs like basil and oregano, or add some unusual ones, such as cilantro, lemon balm, or garlic chives. If you have the space, small varieties of tomatoes, peppers, and even string beans can be grown right in your apartment. Some people have even managed to grow tubs of new potatoes, baby carrots and other root vegetables indoors. Avoid climbing plants, bushy varieties, and plants that take up a lot of space.

It's easy to make your indoor gardening organic. Just don't use fertilizer, pesticides, or other chemicals, and choose seeds from organic sources. Since indoor gardens don't suffer much from pests, molds, or weeds, it's easy to do without the extra chemicals that farms or a big outdoor garden might need. Check on your organic indoor gardening progress regularly to make sure your plants getting enough light and water, however. Plants living in containers take more water than those planted in the ground, and can dry up quickly. Not enough light, and your tomatoes can become spindly, your basil thin, and your peppers will drop their flowers without ever fruiting. A little care, however, and you'll soon be able to enjoy the fruits of your efforts. Plus, you'll know they're good for you!

GROWING CABBAGE IN YOUR ORGANIC GARDEN

Cabbage is a crop that thrives in cool weather. It can be planted in most areas as an early and late season crop. It is grown for it's densely packed leafy head and can be easily growing in your home vegetable garden

It is a crop that prefers full sun, but will tolerate partial shade. The soil conditions that cabbage prefers is a rich soil with a good healthy structure that retains moisture, drains well and can retain the nutrients needed for the plants to thrive. Good soil structure is the key to any successful organic garden. The ph level that is best for it is 6.0 - 6.5. It is a heavy feeder and will be greatly benefited if bron, calcium and magnesium are applied for the early stages of growth.

Cabbage seeds can be sown directly into the garden or started indoors for transplants. When planting transplants in the garden they can go outdoors as early as four weeks before the last expected frost, spaced 6 to 12 inches apart and in rows 1 to 2 feet apart. The spacing of the transplants farther apart will make for the production of bigger heads, but smaller heads are

24

much taster and tender. When sowing seeds indoors set the seeds in your potting media about 1/4 inch deep and about 2 inches apart, place them in a warm sunny location that the temperature is between 60 and 70 degrees Fahrenheit.

When your crop is ready to be harvested it is best to cut the heads when they are firm from the stem and leaving the stem and root in place. They will produce a small cabbage that can also be harvested to eat, like Brussels Sprouts.

A environment friendly and healthy way of gardening. Organic Gardening is away of gardening in harmony with nature. Growing a healthy and productive crop in a way that is healthier for both you and the environment.

GROW WATERMELONS ON DECORATIVE GARDEN OBELISKS

Don't limit your garden obelisks to supporting just flowering vines. Put them to use in your vegetable garden, supporting any of a number of fruiting vines that are grown in home vegetable gardens.

Single serving size watermelons are ideal for vertical growing, whether on decorative obelisks, trellises, arbors or on more functional and utilitarian vegetable garden support structures.

A hot-weather-loving crop that is native to Africa, watermelons (Citrullus spp.) need long, hot summers to develop their sugars and characteristic sweetness. Get a jump on the season, especially in colder northern areas by starting seeds of watermelon indoors.

If you're growing seedless watermelons, you must plant a regular seeded watermelon variety alongside them to pollinate the seedless variety, otherwise they will not produce any fruit.

Plant a seeded variety that looks vastly different from your seedless variety for easier identification.

HERE IS PLANTING INFORMATION TO GUIDE YOU AS YOU PLANT YOUR WATERMELON SEEDS OR TRANSPLANTS:

START SEEDS INDOORS

Start watermelon seeds indoors about 3 weeks before frost-free weather in your area. Plant 2 to 3 seeds in 2 inch peat pots filled with a loose, friable seed starting mixture. Thin to the strongest plant for single transplants or leave the strongest two for transplant "pairs." Grow under artificial lights at temperatures between 80 and 85 degrees Fahrenheit.

Begin to harden off the seedlings on the date of your average last spring frost. Put them outdoors in the shade for a day or two and bring them indoors at night. Then begin moving them into the sun for a longer period each day until they are in the sun all day long. Bring them indoors at night if temperatures threaten to dip below 60 degrees Fahrenheit. Plant in garden about 7 to 10 days after your last spring frost.

Install your decorative garden structure before planting seeds or transplants of watermelons so you do not disturb the tiny seedlings.

DIRECT SEED IN GARDEN

Plant watermelon seeds in the garden after the date of your average last spring frost. Sow the seeds in hills spaced about 4 feet apart in all directions. When the seedlings are about 6 inches high and well established, thin to the strongest three plants in each hill.

PLANT TRANSPLANTS IN GARDEN

Watermelon transplants can be set singly about 2 to 3 feet apart in all directions, or in pairs, with the pairs set about 4 to 5 feet apart in all directions. Warm the soil by covering it with black plastic two to three weeks prior to your last spring frost. Cut "X's" into the black plastic and plant the plants through the resulting openings. Water the watermelon transplants with an all purpose water-soluble fertilizer as you plant them in the garden.

ORGANIC GARDENING - GROWING ONIONS IN YOU HOME VEGETABLE GARDEN

One of the oldest know vegetables is the onion. It is commonly used in a variety of recipes in the kitchens around the world and can be purchased in many different way, from fresh, canned, chopped, dehydrated, frozen and even pickled.

Growing onions can be done from seed, transplants or sets. When choosing seed to start your onions, you will have a larger choice of what you can plant, but can take five months for the seedlings to mature enough to be transplanted and they are more susceptible to disease.

Transplants are onion plants that were started from seed that same season. They can be purchased at some local garden centers, depending on where you live and can be purchased from on line sources. They are usually sold in bunches. They have a shorter growing season than seeds do but can have the same problems like disease.

Sets are the most common way that onions are planted in the home garden and are sold at most local garden centers. They are no more than an immature bulb. These sets are started from seed by sowing the seeds tightly together to create a very thick, tight growing crop of seedlings. This results in a stunted plant growth that will produce a small bulb. These small bulbs is what is sold as sets to be planted the next growing season. When purchasing your sets, keep in mind that they should be about 1/2 inch in diameter and solid, soft small bulbs will not produce a good mature onion, even over size sets that are bigger than 1/2 inch usually wont do good.

When choosing the variety of onion you want to grow, there is one thing that needs to be considered. Onions have what is called day length requirements. Some need 13 to 16 hours of daylight and others only need 12 hours. Choose a variety that is best suitable for your area.

Onions will grow best in a raised garden bed with a good healthy soil structure and plenty of compost or composted manure mixed in and drains well. The soil should have a fairly neutral ph level of between 6 and7.When planting seeds the soil needs to be fluffy or very loose.

Sow seeds directly into the garden bed thickly and cover with a 1/2 inch of fine soil. If you mix radish seeds in the same area they will serve two purposes, deter root maggots and help mark the area where the onion seeds were planted. Once the seedlings start to grow you can start to thin them to about 1 inch apart and then in about a month thin them to 6 inches apart. When you thin them this second time you will want to pull back some of the soil around the bulb to expose the top and sides, this is a great way to induce the development of the bulb.

When planting transplants you want to space then 4 to 6 inches apart and about 2 inches deep.If you are planning on harvesting the onions young then you will want to use the closer 4 inch spacing.

Sets are the third method of planting onions. When purchasing sets you can figure that one pound is enough to plant a fifty foot row. Trench your rows out about 2 inches deep and place the sets with the stem end up. This is the one thing that you will need to watch for when planting. Once you have the sets in place cover with a good garden soil and maintain then with the same methods as transplants.

Time to get ready to harvest your onions is when you see the tops start to turn yellow. At this time you want to bend the greens over horizontally, this will stop the sap from flowing through the stem and put all the plants energy into the maturing bulb. A couple days after you do this you will see the tips starting to turn brown, it is time to pull the onion bulbs from the ground. Do this on a sunny day and lay the bulbs on the ground to dry. When laying the out cover the bulbs by laying the bulbs in a row and covering the next row with the greens . This will help to prevent sun scalding.

A environment friendly and healthy way of gardening. Organic Gardening is away of gardening in harmony with nature. Growing a healthy and productive crop in a way that is healthier for both you and the environment.

CHAPTER 4
BEST PLANTS FOR URBAN GARDENS

Urban gardening may seem like just another trend, but unlike a lot of fads, it's a trend that has staying power because it actually provides substantial benefits to the average person's quality of life. Even apartment dwellers who live several stories up and have nothing more than a small balcony can grow a variety of plants. A small investment in potting soil, growing containers, fertilizer and seeds or starts is all that is needed to create an urban garden.

MAKING THE PATIO OR BALCONY INTO AN URBAN OASIS

Some people desire to be surrounded by lush, blooming vegetation and blossoms and decide to grow flowers in pots on their balconies or their patios. All annual flowers are good choices for this. Those with balcony railings may select vining ornamental plants that will grow around the railings. Good choices for this include nasturtiums, morning glories, blue potato vine and even rambling roses. Not many things are better after a tough day in an office than relaxing with a cocktail or glass of sweet tea at a table in your own outdoor living space. Annual flowers have the benefit of providing blooms for an extended period of time, providing color from spring through autumn.

CULINARY HERBS FOR A CITY APARTMENT

Many people who live in the city are discovering the satisfaction of creating meals in their own homes rather than constantly eating takeout or going to restaurants. A patio or balcony is the perfect place to grow culinary herbs in pots. Herbs generally don't take much fertilizer and only require an adequate amount of watering, and they are often aromatic. Meals taste much better when prepared with fresh herbs. Oregano, chives, mint, rosemary, sage and lemon balm are just few example of culinary herbs that can be successfully grown in pots, and some can even be grown on sunny windowsills during the winter months.

VEGETABLE GARDENS IN URBAN YARDS

People who live in houses within city limits are increasingly choosing to forgo lawn space in favor of vegetable gardens. Tomatoes, corn, lettuce, radishes, beets, spinach and broccoli are a few of the items that grow well in home gardens. Various salad greens can be grown together in large containers and picked when fresh salads are needed. Although the back yard is the traditional domain of home gardens, people are beginning to see the value in using their front yards for growing vegetables as well. Those who have consumed meals prepared with vegetables from home gardens are rarely satisfied with grocery store produce.

BRINGING THE COUNTRY TO THE CITY

Incorporating plant life into an urban environment has emotional, nutritional and aesthetic benefits. No matter how small their apartment or house, city dwellers can always find a way to grow herbs, vegetables or ornamental flowers in containers or on small patches of land. Some even grow fruit trees in large outdoor planters. Cherry tomatoes do especially well when planted in hanging baskets.

People who live in apartments or condos with no outdoor space available at all can still grow herbs and flowers indoors. Grow lights and hydroponic systems are available for those who want to do this. With advancements in horticultural technology, there is no reason why those living in even the deepest urban pockets can't have an abundance of vegetation in their lives.

GARDEN FOUNTAINS: A SIGHT TO BEHOLD

There are lots of factors why people enjoy having garden fountains in their homes. In addition to their artistic purposes, fountains serve much more uses than what meets your eyes. In today's hectic world, fountains gives a respite from the hectic lifestyle helping to lessen the pressure we all experience on a daily basis. The soft sound of trickling water brings about a natural tranquilizing and comforting effect, and allows you to take a break and step from all the madness. Whether placed in a sprawling garden or hidden in a cozy nook within the apartment, garden fountains alleviate life's tension in some ways.

Several homeowners with plenty of space in their yards go through the process of employing professional landscapers to make garden fountains which feature intricate and unusual designs to catch the owner's creative whims. They get ideas from popular garden fountains seen in different parts of the world. Others let their imaginations make the reins and choose designs that differ from modern minimalist to outrageously fancy and luxurious. These kinds of garden fountains are considered art pieces and form a centrifugal point in the well-manicured lawn that draws special interest.

But having a small space is not an excuse for other homeowners from making their own corner of paradise. People residing in high-rise apartments can also put together small garden fountains right in their comfy crib. There are lots of do-it-yourself garden fountains available in the market today. These kits come complete with an electric water pump and hose (blank) to allow water cascade freely. The fun part in creating these small fountains lay in setting up materials together that will make up the overall design. Owners are left with a freehand to create their very own style making use of materials they fancy and then the result often turn out to be more than amazing. Another advantage of having compact fountains is that these can be moved around easily and can complement practically any re-arrangements around the house.

In addition to their therapeutic effect, fountains likewise bring about some luck into the house based on popular Eastern values. Feng Shui, in particular, considers water as a vital element that can help a steady flow of positive energy, prosperity and good relationships. Feng Shui experts place garden fountains in strategic spots within the house to make sure there's a balance of energy that moves through it. Even large Chinese-owned institutions and buildings have their own pocket gardens complete with fountains to usher good luck and abundance.

Whatever reason you might have for putting together garden fountains, it must be remembered what water ought to always be kept clean and then the fountain itself be cleansed at least a month based on the type of water used and the place where the fountain is set. Just remember to pay a little extra attention for the outdoor fountains since it requires more maintenance because of its exposure to debris and other dirt that could clog the flow of the water.

PLANNING WHEN TO START YOUR SEEDS FOR YOUR APARTMENT GARDEN

This is the time of year I have to exercise the greatest self control. I've been reading through gardening catalogs, looking through my seed supply and planning what to grow, seeing visions of my beautiful garden. It takes everything I have to not start my seeds too early.

My favorite resource for planning when to start my seeds is the book All New Square Foot Gardening. I highly recommend the book for any gardener, as it has lots of useful information for everyone. Today I'll be looking in the back of the book at the "Crop-by-Crop Guide," which tells how much space a plant needs and when they can be planted and when they can go outside.

To know when to start your plants you'll need to know when the date of your last and first frosts. If you're in the US or Canada you can check Victory Seeds' Frost Date Selector, or ask a fellow gardener who lives near you. According to the chart my last frost should be around May 25th.

I suggest buying, making or printing a calendar to remind you when to plant your seeds and when to do other major things (transplant them, put them outside, etc.). You can put these things on your regular calendar if you wish, but I like having a dedicated gardening one.

Now back to the book. Let's say I want to grow some lettuce.

According to the chart on the lettuce page I can start my seeds seven weeks before the last frost and can be put outside up to four weeks before the last frost. Since I'm pretty far north I probably won't put them outside until a lot closer to the last frost date, and even then I'll have to keep an eye on the weather. Because of that I'll plan on starting my seeds about 5 weeks before the last frost, or around April 20th, which happens to be a Wednesday. I usually have Wednesdays off so that works fine for me, so on the calendar it goes. If the date you come up with doesn't work with your schedule, just pick the closest date you have available.

I definitely want at least one tomato plant this year and the book tells me to start my seeds six weeks before the last frost and to not put them out while there's still a danger of frost. Six weeks before my last frost will be April 13th, the Wednesday before my lettuce needs to be planted. It's good to spread out these tasks so you don't get overwhelmed.

I go on this way until I have figured out when to plant everything I'm planning on growing. The book only covers major vegetables, so for herbs and flowers you'll have to either look up the information online or find it on the seed packets.

While you're looking up it's a good idea to make a list or chart of what size pots each plant will need so you can start collecting them. You don't want to get to transplant day and have no pots!

EASY VEGETABLE GARDEN GROWING FOR APARTMENT LIVING

No longer do people have the luxury of living in homes with a large garden. Many people now live in apartments and condos, but this does not mean that they cannot grow their own vegetables. Surprised? Well, you should not be. Here are a few ideas to get you started successfully on vegetable garden growing for apartment living.

The answer to growing vegetables in an apartment with limited space is container gardening. The first thing that you need to do is check for a spot in your apartment where there is ample sunlight and sufficient space to easily access the containers. Some of the best spots in apartments are the deck, rooftop and also near the windows.

Once you have selected the space for your vegetable garden, the next thing that you should pay attention to is the kind of vegetables and fruits you want to grow. Do not opt for fruits and vegetables just because you have heard that certain ones are easy to grow. You should only select those which you are going to eat. So, if you love to eat tomatoes, then grow tomatoes. Also, here it becomes important to take into account the type of climate the area has. Visit the local nursery to figure out which fruits and vegetables will best grow in your area. Then select the ones that you like eating.

The key to easy vegetable growing for apartment living is ensuring that you do not start big. You are bound to be successful if you have a small container garden with just one or two vegetables to start with. Once you realize that your enthusiasm has not dampened and you are successful as an apartment gardener, you can add more vegetables to your garden. Also, make sure that you grow only amounts that you can eat. In case, you end up with too many vegetables, be a nice neighbor and share your bounty. You can also give the surplus to friends and family.

THE 12 EASIEST VEGETABLES TO GROW IN HOME GARDENS OR CONTAINERS FOR FIRST TIME GARDENERS

A lot of people, myself included, are growing our own vegetables to beat the credit crunch. And why not? Planting a few seeds in containers, in your backyard or in your garden will yield delicious, organic vegetables - and can save money, too! Growing organic vegetables is easier than you think. Here are the 12 vegetables you will have no problem planting, tending for and harvesting in your own garden, even if you are a first-time gardener!

1. RADISH

These are particularly easy to grow and can be intercropped with rows of lettuce to take up a minimum amount of space! Great thing about radishes is that very few pests bother them. Choose a sunny, sheltered position in soil, well fed with organic matter. Sow the seed thinly, evenly at ½ inch below the soil's surface with one inch of space between each. Water the soil thoroughly before sowing and after the seeds emerge water them lightly every couple days. Radishes are a great source of potassium, folic acid, magnesium and calcium, and are perfect in salad dressings or as a garnish for salads. Radishes are fast growers and should be ready to pull in several weeks.

2. ZUCCHINI/ SQUASH

Zucchini and squash do well in most climates and they need very little special attention. If you plant zucchini you'll could end up with way more than they can even eat!

Zucchini and squash are very low in calories but full of potassium, manganese and folate. Sow several zucchini seeds in a heap pile of composted soil a foot high and a couple feet wide. Space each heap pile approximately 3 feet apart, water them heavily every other day and wait for them to sprout in a couple weeks. They should be ready to harvest about a month later. For any early start sow the seeds singly about 1/2 in (1.25cm) deep, in small pots and place in a temperature of 65-70F (18-21C). After germination of seeds, grow on in a well lit spot, harden off and plant out after the last spring frost when the weather is warm.

3. CARROTS

Carrots tend to be pest free and need little attention. Carrots are rich in vitamin A, antioxidants, carotene and dietary. Dig a hole less than an inch deep and plant a couple of seeds in each, and leave several inches in between holes. Thin out in stages to 4-6in (10-15cm) apart. Keep the soil moist but remember to water the carrots less as they begin to reach maturity.

4. SPINACH

A highly nutritious and easily grown crop, high in both calcium and iron. Spinach can be eaten plain, cooked, and made into a chip dip. Turn over the soil with compost and plant seeds less than an inch deep, placing them at least 4 inches apart to give room for growth. Pick young leaves regularly. Sow the soil a couple more times in the first month and keep this area well-watered.

5. PEAS

Peas are another high-yield crop, both sweet peas and sugar peas. Other than fruit flies, these guys attract very few pests. A good source of vitamins A, B and C. Cultivate the soil just prior to sowing top dress with a balanced fertilizer. Keep in mind that your soil must drain well in order for peas for flourish. Space each seed several inches apart and sow them one inch deep. Freshly planted seeds require 1/2 inch of water every week, while more mature plants need a full inch. Any surplus peas can be frozen very successfully.

6. PEPPERS

Peppers contain nutrients like thiamin and manganese. Peppers can be stuffed with meat and rice or used in salsa and pasta, and raw in salads. Till the soil with compost and Epsom salts, this will make it rich in magnesium to help the peppers develop healthily. Peppers can be produced outside in growing bags, large pots etc. Since they grow best in warm soil, sow the seeds a foot or more apart in raised beds or containers. Water them frequently, keeping the soil moist, or they may taste bitter once harvested.

7. LETTUCE/ BABY GREENS

Lettuce is one of the easiest vegetables to grow; you just have to plant the seeds, water and watch how fast it grows. Lettuce is a good source of folic acid and vitamin A, used as the main ingredient mostly in salads, but also can be stuffed with various ingredients to make a lettuce wrap or top sandwiches, hamburgers and tacos. When cultivating the soil with nutrient-rich compost, break up any chunks and remove debris. Make sure that seeds are planted between 8 and 16 inches apart and water them every morning. Avoid doing so at night because this could cause disease. Loose-leaf varieties are ready to start cutting about seven weeks after sowing.

Baby greens are simply greens that are harvested while they are still young and tender. They are true instant gratification vegetables - you'll be harvesting your first salad in under a month! Sprinkle the seeds as thinly as possible across the soil in a 2- to 3-inch wide band. Space rows of baby greens 6 to 8 inches apart. Or plant baby greens in a pot, and cut your salad fresh every night!

8. ONION

Rich in dietary fiber, folate and vitamin C, onion need little care - just give them plenty of water. Plow the soil a foot deep and get rid of debris. The easiest way to grow onions is from sets which are small onions. Plant sets so that the tip is showing about 5in (13cm) apart in rows 12in (30cm) apart. Or, plant the seeds a couple centimeters deep and several inches apart. Weed this area frequently but gently and provide them with about an inch of water every week.

9. BEETS

Beets (beetroots) can be peeled, steamed, and then eaten warm with butter; cooked, pickled, and then eaten cold as a condiment; or peeled, shredded raw, and then eaten as a salad.. Betanin, one of the primary nutrients in this deep red or purple vegetable, can help lower blood pressure. Clean and strengthen the seeds by soaking them in water at room temperature for a day. Plow the soil and remove any stones from the top 3 feet. Plant each seed 2in (5cm) apart, thin out to 4in (10cm) apart and water them at least once every day.

10. BROCCOLI

For the most part doesn't need a lot of special care, broccoli is easily grown vegetable that gives the best return for the space it occupies and is cropped when other green vegetables are in short supply. One row of 15ft (4.5m) will accommodate six plants to give self-sufficiency for a family of four. Sow broccoli seed in spring in a seed bed ½in (1.25cm) deep and transplant when the seedlings are about 4in (10cm) tall 2ft (60cm) apart each way.

11. TOMATOES

There are many benefits to growing tomatoes - they're tasty, they9re good for you, and the dollar value of the yield can be very significant. Tomatoes are rich in nutrients like niacin, potassium and phosphorous, antioxidants like lycopene, anthocyanin and carotene, and vitamins A, C and E.

Sow the seed just below the surface in a tray of peat-based compost. When the seedlings have made two pairs of true leaves prick them out into 3in (7.5cm) pots and place them in a light, warm place indoors (like windowsill). After the last danger of frost has passed, pick a spot in your garden that receives at least 6-8 hours of sunlight and test the soil's pH level - it needs to be between 6 and 7. (To decrease pH level add sulfur, to increase it add lime). Spread compost over this area and mix it with the soil. After hardening off, set tomato plants 2ft (60cm) apart in rows 3ft (90cm) apart, bush plants 3ft (90cm) apart. Water them a couple times per week.

Tomatoes do need a little more attention then the other vegetables on the list. However, for the little bit attention that tomatoes do need, you get an incredible reward in the large amount of fruit that they produce. To help you get started, here is a complete guide to growing tomatoes

12. HERBS

There are many herbs including thyme, rosemary, basil, mint, sage, chives, parsley and oregano that need very little attention and can be grown successfully in containers on a patio, balcony or terrace. Purchase some of your favorite small herb plants from your local nursery and get a container that is at least 6-12 inches deep. You can plant multiple herbs in a wide or long container or use at least a 6" pot for individual plants and you will enjoy not only their fragrance and beauty but also their culinary benefits. Water sparingly because herbs don't like to sit in wet soil.

If you are a first time gardener, start slow with any of the vegetables I've mentioned. Soon, you will gain confidence and have a beautiful organic vegetable garden!

APARTMENT GARDENS: NOURISHING YOUR PLANTS

You love planting small flowers in your small home garden, but there's a huge dilemma - your apartment or house receives little sunlight or you have barely enough room to nourish your plants. As a result of the poor lighting, your plants are turning up dead or not growing at all, while the space is making it difficult to grow several plants. In spite of these poor conditions, you are determined to start your own garden and grow your favorite plants and vegetables, so you improvise the location and even contemplate using a grow room setup to nourish your plants. If you find yourself feeling hopeless, never fear because you can still start your garden, but you'll just have to make a few creative selections.

LIMITED SPACE, NO PROBLEM

Scanning your home or apartment, you see how packed the area is, making it difficult to start a garden. Yes, space may be an issue, but you can get rid of various unnecessary products on your apartment balcony and use plant containers to jump start your project. Depending on your geographic place and the setup of your apartment, it is practical to start a miniature home garden utilizing container gardening. Container gardening functions as a pain-free alternative to needing soil to plant flowers or vegetables in. The flowers, vegetables and fruits you set inside the containers can still prosper, you just need to ensure there are drainage holes and there is sufficient soil to support the plant. Please note, containers can come in the form of plastic pots built for plants or improvised plastic containers; so long as the plant has plenty of water and light, it will mature. Be confident, as it will allow your creativity to glow, allowing you to adorn your window ledge or balcony with flair. Since flower pots come in several styles and sizes, you are bound to find the right pot for the living location.

CERTAIN PLANTS ARE NOT MADE FOR APARTMENTS

Remember, some flowers, fruits and vegetables you'll want to steer clear of as they are either too hefty for a small environment or are very difficult to care for. For instance, watermelon, lettuce and sunflowers. These plants are tasty to eat and a marvel to look at, but the difficulty witnessed when trying to plant with limited space makes it hard to imagine that they can be raised in such an environment. You need area to grow some kinds of flowers, vegetables and fruits and a container may not be enough. You want to pay attention to smaller plants and flowers that require little space, such as daisies, tulips, carrots and even peppers.

LIMITED LIGHT, NO PROBLEM

The largest reason why most apartment renters cannot start a garden is the limited light located in their apartment; little light makes it difficult to start a home garden. For people looking to grow fruits or vegetables, plants require at least six hours or more of light. Do not forget that plants do not require light from just the sun; they can also get the essential light from led grow lights, which make it possible for you to grow them indoors. If you are afraid of the large electric bill that may come from grow lights, don't worry because these lights are both relatively inexpensive and use up little electrical power.

APARTMENT GARDENING - TIPS FOR GROWING VEGETABLES IN CONTAINERS

Can you have your own vegetable garden if you live in an apartment with tight spaces? Absolutely! Growing vegetables in containers is the answer for gardening enthusiasts who do not have space for a garden in their home. Think of your balcony, window sill, patio or even a bright, sunny corner in your living room. All these are potential locations for creating your indoor vegetable garden..

Container vegetable gardening is becoming popular not simply because it has made it possible for apartment dwellers to have their own piece of green sanctuary. Even gardeners who have an outdoor garden are also getting into container gardening for the following reasons:

1. Portability makes it easy to arrange the plants
2. Effective control over the spread of diseases across different plants.
3. Ability to personalize your little garden with a variety of containers
4. No need to repair the lawn if the plants don't work out

These are just some of the reasons that encourage garden owners to get into container gardening. It doesn't matter if you are having your container vegetable garden indoors or outdoors, there are some golden rules of growing vegetables in containers that will help improve your success rate in vegetable gardening.

GOLDEN RULES FOR GROWING VEGETABLES IN CONTAINERS

1. CHOOSING A CONTAINER

Before you embark on your shopping spree to purchase gardening supplies, ask yourself - what kind of vegetables do I want to plant? Being clear about what you want to plant will give you a better idea of the type of containers you should be buying. If you are going for big plants, you will need bigger, deeper containers that provide space for the development of strong roots.

Generally, it is recommended to use bigger containers for vegetable gardening. You should take both the diameter and depth of the container into consideration. For vegetable plants to be robust and healthy, deep containers are needed as it has more room for roots to develop a strong foundation. The material which the pots and containers are made of is not as important. Plastic, terra cotta and timber planters are all suitable for growing vegetables. Just note that size and depth are more important.

If you plan to grow vegetables such as peppers, tomatoes, spinach, zucchini, lettuce and cucumbers, a 3-5 gallon container will be sufficient. Larger containers of 15 gallon will be needed for the bigger plants.

2. LOCATION OF YOUR CONTAINER

The availability of sunlight is a main consideration when it comes to positioning your container vegetable plants. Ensure that your vegetable plants get sufficient sunlight if you want to have healthy plants and a good harvest. Majority of vegetable plants, particularly beans, peppers and tomatoes need a good 6 to 8 hours of sunlight daily.

The location of your containers plays an important part to the survival of your vegetable plants. Apart from sunlight, you also have to consider if the location is windy. Strong winds tend to dry up plants; hence you should avoid positioning your container plants at windy areas. If you are unable to avoid the strong winds, you can construct a windbreaker around your vegetable plants to shield them.

Catering ample space between the containers is just as crucial as it provides good air circulation for your plants. When positioning your containers, ensure that the taller plants do not shade out the shorter ones. In this way, all of your plants will have an equal chance of exposure to sunlight.

3. CHOOSING SOIL TYPE

Using the right kind of soil will provide your vegetable plants with a good foundation for strong growth. Heavy potting soil or garden soil is not suitable for growing vegetables in containers. A better choice would be container mix that has better moisture retention capability and can resist compaction. You can also consider creating your own compost with manure added. This is probably a better option than buying ready made garden soil from the nursery.

Do take note of the vegetable type as well when you are selecting the soil. Potatoes prefer rich, loamy soil while carrots prefer sandier, more free-draining compost.

4. WATERING

Container plants tend to absorb more heat, hence they often take in quite a bit of water. It is crucial that you water your container vegetable plants frequently to prevent them from drying up. Take this into consideration when positioning your containers. Easy access to water points will make it more convenient for frequent watering.

How do you know if your plant has enough water? First and foremost, you have to determine the moisture level of the soil. Your container plants should not have soaking wet soil as it can result in rotting roots. Use the finger test to determine the moisture level of the soil. Dip your index finger into the soil. If the soil feels hard and dry, you got to water your plants. If the surface, or just below the surface of the soil feels moist, you can water your plants the next day.

If you don't want to use the finger test, get a soil moisture meter to do the job. In fact, this is a more precise approach than the finger test to measure soil moisture level.

5. ADDING FERTILIZERS

Since container plants require frequent watering, the fertilizer will get diluted faster too. You should feed your container vegetable plants with fertilizers twice as often. Doing so will ensure your plants of a healthy supply of fertilizers for strong and healthy growth.

Growing vegetables in containers at home allows you to enjoy fresh home-grown vegetables at any time. Nothing beats the satisfaction of being able to savor the fruits of your labor and to share it with your loved ones. Indoor vegetable gardening is such a pleasure when you have the know-how and tips to grow a bountiful harvest.

HEAT UP YOUR CONTAINER GARDEN WITH HOT PEPPERS

Hot peppers seem to be a favorite among many gardeners - almost as popular as tomatoes and with fans just as dedicated. Each year gardeners try to outdo each other by growing the hottest pepper in the world, or at least on their block. These blisteringly hot creations can make pepper spray seem tame. Whether you're looking for something as hot as the sun or just a little heat to add to your food, hot peppers are just the thing.

Unlike many vegetables, peppers often do better in containers than in the ground. The reason is because peppers like warm soil, and a container sitting in the sun can heat up pretty quickly. You can use your pepper containers to block the sun from plants that don't like warm soil to keep everyone happy. Some temperature extremes can cause problems for peppers.

They like temperatures of at least 70F but not over 90F during the day and above 60F at night to set flowers (note - the soil temperature is more important than the air temperature, so if your temperatures are a little high or low you'll probably be fine). If the temperatures get too far out of that range they may drop their blossoms until the temperatures get back into their comfort range.

Pretty much any hot pepper will do well in a container. Some or the most popular hot peppers that work well in containers are habaneros, jalapenos, cayenne, Thai Dragon and Hungarian hot wax. They can be started from seed or purchased from your local nursery. If starting from seed I recommended not using peat pellets or peat pots as these can cause problems and keep the roots too wet. Many people have had good luck with peat, but the results seem pretty mixed. If you can keep the seeds warm with a heat mat or by keeping them near a radiator they will sprout more quickly.

Peppers like a light, quick draining soil. Make sure your pots have plenty of drainage and a suitable potting soil or mix. If you want to make your own, a popular recipe calls for 5 parts orchid bark (actually made from softwood trees, usually fir), 1 part potting mix, 1 part perlite and a tablespoon of dolomitic garden lime. This will provide quick drainage and the right pH for your peppers. Even with quick draining soil, be careful not to over-water your peppers. Consistency is the key, as inconsistent watering can cause blossom end rot and other problems.

You'll want some fairly large containers to grow your peppers. For varieties that grow no more than 12 inches tall you can get away with a two gallon pot. For larger peppers a five to ten gallon container is recommended. If you have an even larger space you can plant more than one pepper, but make sure you don't over-crowd them, they like their space.

Peppers may or may not need some form of support, depending on the variety, size and how productive they are. Use your best judgment in deciding what to use and when. Most people prefer stakes and only support the main stem, but cages and other techniques can work better in some situations.

You can keep your peppers producing all season by harvesting the fruits as they get to eatable size. Harvest them by cutting the stem rather than pulling the peppers off. If you let the peppers sit on the plant too long the plant will figure its work is done for the year and not make any more peppers.

Speaking of harvesting peppers, there are some precautions to take when growing and handling hot peppers. I suggest wearing disposable rubber gloves when harvesting, or at least make sure you wash your hands VERY well after handling. Either way be very careful not to touch your eyes after touching peppers. Be careful with children and pets around hot peppers. People and animals brushing against hot peppers can transfer capsaicin (the ingredient in peppers that makes them burn) to their skin or clothing, which can cause a burning rash or can be accidentally transferred to their eyes, which is a very unpleasant thing (trust me on this one!).

Hot peppers are a great way to add visual appeal to a garden with their colors and shapes. I hope you'll give some a try!

CHAPTER 5
EARLY PLANT COMBINATIONS FOR INTENSIVE GARDENING BEDS

Using a planning template for the 4' intensive gardening beds, where a similar main crop will be occupying the center row. The second bed can be planned with similar crops in the center nine rows, and the outside two rows changed, to provide more variety.

Both intensive gardening beds can be planted at the same time. Peas and spinach can't be planted in very many successions because they need to grow to maturity while it remains cool; therefore they will harvest at the same time and be finished for the year unless you plan for a fall crop. Planning multiple beds is a good way to get your spinach and Pea food storage, and fresh use lettuce, beets, green onions and carrots.

The outside row crops can be planted in successions mixed in beds with other plant types. For carrot and beet food storage they turn out better if planted later in the season. In my location in Utah I would normally start planting the beds March 15.

BED NUMBER ONE MARCH 15

SR 1 Lettuce Thin to 12" apart and use thins.
SR 2 Spinach Thin to 3" apart and use thins.
MR 1 Spinach Thin to 3" apart and use thins.
SR 3 Bush Peas No thinning necessary.

SR 4 Bush Peas No thinning necessary.

CR Spinach Transplant Tomatoes May 1, 2' apart

SR 5 Bush Peas No thinning necessary.

SR 6 Bush Peas No thinning necessary.

MR 2 Spinach Thin to 3" apart and use thins.

SR 7 Spinach Thin to 3" apart and use thins.

SR 8 Green Onions Thin to 3" apart and use thins.

BED NUMBER TWO MARCH 15

SR 1 Beets Thin to 6" apart and use thins.

SR 2 Spinach Thin to 3" apart and use thins.

MR 1 Spinach Thin to 3" apart and use thins.

SR 3 Bush Peas No thinning necessary.

SR 4 Bush Peas No thinning necessary.

CR Spinach Transplant Tomatoes May 1, 2' apart

SR 5 Bush Peas No thinning necessary.

SR 6 Bush Peas No thinning necessary.

MR 2 Spinach Thin to 3" apart and use thins.

SR 7 Spinach Thin to 3" apart and use thins.

SR 8 Carrots Thin to 3" apart and use thins.

The SR 1 and SR 8 can also be planted with swiss chard, kohl rabi, or other plants that fit into the same category. When more tomatoes are wanted for that year, and you have the space available, you can plant another bed with other plant types in SR 1 and SR 8. That is a good way to get your tomato food storage.

The spinach in all of the SR can be substituted for turnips, but the turnips will be thinned to 6". The MR 1, and MR 2 would need to be left unplanted with that combination. The spinach from the CR in the above plan will be thinned, and will be large enough to eat when the tomato plants are transplanted. The rest of the spinach in that row will be harvested before the peas and tomatoes need the space.

The tomato cages will need to be set in place before the peas get over 6" tall. All of the spinach or turnips will be harvested from the bed first, followed by the peas. The pea vines will die and will be removed. The SR 1 and SR 8 crops will harvest next and you will have tomatoes harvesting from that bed for the rest of the season. Twelve full rows of vegetables will ultimately be harvested from a 4' intensive garden bed with the above planting combination.

When planting four rows of peas like this bed plan the only CR plant that will not be affected by the shading, are tomatoes. Peas do well planted in multiple rows, they help support each other, and are not too hard to harvest when they are grown that way.

Tomatoes can be eliminated from the CR in this planting combination, the center row can be planted later with a fall crop of broccoli, cauliflower etc. Then the other SR's can be planted with more carrots, beets, or other plants that do not have to be harvested to make room for the tomatoes. Do not put swiss chard, green onions or other longer season plants in that combination, or they will still be growing when you want to plant the fall crop.

Keep in mind that this tomato bed combination can be repeated every two weeks three more times, providing successions of early crops, and will add a row for tomatoes each time. You will need a lot more space to do this, or design your beds shorter so that you have more beds to work with.

Below is another good intensive gardening bed combination to use for the next succession planting and the main crop of peppers, or other main crops.

BED NUMBER THREE APRIL 1

SR 1 Lettuce Thin to 12" apart and use thins.

SR 2 Spinach Thin to 3" apart and use thins.

MR 1 Spinach Transplant Peppers May 1, 2' apart

SR 3 Spinach Thin to 3" apart and use thins.

SR 4 Spinach Thin to 3" apart and use thins.

CR Spinach Transplant Peppers May 1, 2' apart

SR 5 Spinach Thin to 3" apart and use thins.

SR 6 Spinach Thin to 3" apart and use thins.

MR 2 Spinach Transplant Peppers May 1, 2' apart

SR 7 Spinach Thin to 3" apart and use thins.

SR 8 Green Onions Thin to 3" apart and use thins.

The SR 1 and SR 8 are planted the same as the bed one example, all of the other SR's need to be spinach, turnips etc. The space will be needed later for the three rows of peppers.

The CR can also be used for eggplants. The eggplants are larger plants and will work best in the CR. This bed combination will be good for your cole crops also. Plant the CR with broccoli, brussel sprouts, celery etc. MR 1 and MR 2 can be planted with cabbage, cauliflower etc. You can mix the cabbage up with red, early, mid, late-season varieties, and even bok choy or kale.

Try to have one family of plants as the main crop in each bed, since each family of plants will have different needs. Some plants are heavy feeders, some are light feeders, and some actually feed nitrogen back into the soil. Some plants need more nitrogen, some more potassium, and some more potash. There are also some plants that prefer alkaline conditions, some acid, and some in between.

For the best sharing of the fertilizer crop rotation will be important to practice. Another plant group next year will use what nutrients the plant group from this year didn't use. The next year another plant group will help build the soil.

With intensive gardening it will always be necessary to keep adding organic matter to the beds. Crop rotation alone will not be enough because the demand on the soil is too great, and it is important for disease and insect control to maintain healthy soil. Healthy soil makes healthy plants.

SOME FAVORITE GARDEN BULBS

Bulbs are a great addition to any garden as they will provide color year after year and can even provide additional flowers to be divided and planted in another part of the garden. Unlike, annuals, bulb flowers do not need to be planted each year.

Bulbs are hardy in nature and there is a color, shape or size that should suit any gardening need. Here's some favorite garden bulbs and their planting needs.

CROCUS

Crocus bulbs are often the fist blooms we see in early spring or at the end of winter. Their tubular shaped flowers range in size from 1½" to 3" long. Crocuses are planting in almost every garden and have a wide range of colors to suite any taste. Other types of crocus, such as the saffron crocus, bloom instead in the fall, and the flowers can rise from the bare ground weeks, or even only days, after the bulbs are planted. Crocus bulbs should be planted in the fall. Plant the bulbs 2 to 3 inches deep and space 3 or 4 inches apart. Crocuses require well drained soil, regular watering and will grow in full sun or partial shade.

DAHLIA

Dahlias have a long bloom time from summer through fall and like many other bulbs come in a large variety of colors, sizes and shapes.

These flowers are so diverse that there are varieties with flower sizes ranging from 2 to 12 inches and from under a foot to 7 feet tall! Plant dahlias in spring after threat of frost has passed. Plant between 4 and 6 inches deep with spacing of 1 foot for short varieties and 5 feet for the tall variety's. Dahlias like full sun unless you are planting them in a very hot climate where they might do well with a little shade. As with most flowers, make sure these are watered regularly.

GALANTHUS NIVALIS

This plant is more commonly called the snowdrop and is one of the first plants to bloom after winter. They are short plants about 6 inches tall and have two bell shaped flowers. They thrive in colder climates. Plant snowdrops in fall, dig down 3 to 4 inches and plant 3 inches apart. These flowers like full sun but will tolerate partial shade. Water regularly during the growing cycle.

DAFFODIL

The daffodil may be the most easily recognizable of all bulb plants, and it rewards its gardener with a generous display of beautiful blooms. Besides the traditional white and yellow varieties, daffodils also come in shades of orange, apricot, pink and cream. Daffodil bulbs should be planted twice as deep as they are tall, and they should be spaced between six and eight inches apart. Daffodils benefit from full sun and regular watering during their growth and bloom periods.

TULIP

Tulips are a favorite flower around the world and one of the most easy to recognize. These are among the most hybridized of all flowers, with hybrids available in a staggering array of shapes, sizes, colors and textures. Tulips bloom from mid spring to late spring with different varieties having different bloom times. Tulips should be planted in fall and each bulb should be planted about 3 times deeper than the size of the bulb.A 2" wide bulb would be planted 6" deep. It is important to leave sufficient space between the planted bulbs as well, from four to eight inches depending on the size of the bulb.

GLADIOLUS

Gladiolas are among the most popular of all bulb plants, and their distinctive sword shaped leaves and funnel shaped flowers are instantly recognizable to gardeners and non gardeners alike. Gladiolas are best planted in the spring, but only after the soil has warmed. Gladiolas do best in full sunlight and they should be watered regularly during their blooming and growth phase. In much of the country, gladiola bulbs can be left in the ground over the winter months, but many gardeners choose to dig them up and store them during the winter. If you decide to take this approach, it is best to dig them after the leaves have turned yellow. The bulbs should be placed in a single layer and stored in a cool, dry and dark place to dry for two or three weeks. After the bulbs have dried sufficiently they should be stored in nylon stockings or onion sacks and kept in a cool and well ventilated place.

HEMEROCALLIS

Hemerocallis is the scientific name for the daylily, and it is one of the most well known types of bulb plants on the market. Daylily hybrids can grow as tall as six feet and bloom in the spring and summer months. The daylily produces flowers ranging in size from three to eight inches, and they are available in a wide variety of colors. The daylily is actually a tuberous root variety of bulb, and they are best planted during fall or early spring. Daylilies should be planted between ½ inch and 1 inch deep and space between 2 to 2½ inches apart in the garden. As with other varieties of bulbs, it is important to water daylilies on a regular basis during their growing season.

HYACINTHS (DUTCH HYACINTH)

The Dutch hyacinth is one of the most instantly recognizable, and most popular, of all the varieties of bulb plants. The Dutch hyacinth blooms in the spring and features the well known foot high spires with their small bell shaped and very fragrant flowers. Hyacinths come in a wide varieties of colors, including red, pink, buff, white, blue and purple. The Dutch hyacinth grows best in colder areas, and it can last from year to year. In these cold water climates, the hyacinth is best planted in September of October. It is best to plant hyacinth bulbs four to five inches deep, and to space them from four to five inches apart as well. Hyacinths grow best in full sunlight, and they benefit from regular watering, especially during their blooming and growth periods.

IRIS

The most frequently seen variety of irises are the bearded varieties. Bearded irises are striking plants, and they appear in a dazzling array of colors and combinations of colors. Irises appear in a variety of sizes as well, with very small varieties and very large ones as well. Irises should be planted in July or August in cold climates and in September or October in warmer areas. Irises are actually rhizomes, and they should be spaced from one to two feet apart, with the tops placed right below the surface of the soil. Irises grow best in full sunlight or light shade, and they benefit from a regular watering schedule during their growing season.

CHAPTER 6
EVERY GREAT BACHELOR PAD SHOULD HAVE A GREAT GARDEN

Unless you're under 35 or over 65 you might not have noticed that there's been an explosion in city living. London apartment developments have been popping up all over the capital fed by a growing need for neat single living units and a desire to be where the action is, and at the most within a night bus home.

In the UK some 50% of new homes are apartments, a trend that's found worldwide, and this has led to some unusual trends in garden design and gardening. In particular it has led to gardens on a tiny scale with a new trend in micro gardening including vertical green walls and grow your own. Community gardening in these new neighbourhoods is a big trend that we're hearing about. But one trend that has gone under the radar is the rise of slick independent male apartment living - old style bachelor pads with a new twist. They want a garden to match their stylish new homes.

The rise of these new bachelor pad gardens is led by a few different influences. First of all there is a new sophistication for staying home and if you are entertaining your date then what better than taking them out into your stylish outdoor space, sitting around a fireplace at night time whatever the season. Second climate change in city centres has led to more exotic gardening, if you have a warm micro climate in your London garden then you can grow exotic plants like luxurious tree ferns and sexy jungle plants like canna lilies.

The other big influence is technology, serious boys toys for the garden. New LED lighting technology gives a great atmosphere year round and even when it snows what better view than a snow lit landscape. But of course night time garden lighting allows busy city boys to relax in the garden when they get home, have a beer from their slick stainless steel cooling drawer and chill out. Add in a great sound system linked into the internal computerised music feed and an outdoor TV and you've got an extension to your small apartment for year round entertainment.

A challenge for every small city garden is seclusion, especially if you're a bachelor entertaining his latest girl or boyfriend. It doesn't have to be the usual timber fence and the contemporary horizontal trellis that has sprung up in suburban gardens isn't enough when your home displays your tastes to people you want to impress.

And plants are just as important to create that secluded atmosphere. In small gardens every plant counts and it's important to choose wisely. For the gardener he might sacrifice seating space for planting but for many it's about low maintenance garden design that means occasional gardening whilst enjoying great simple planting schemes with a peak of interest for the summertime. For the minimalist bachelor pad it might mean a single great Japanese Maple but the clear white branches of multi-stem birches and black bamboo are a popular choice. For the single male interested in emanating Gordon Ramsey or Jamie Oliver there's also an interest in planting more unusual exotic edibles like Szechuan pepper or

Cocktail Kiwis that thrive in the warmth of the city.

Whatever their taste for planting and gardening there seems to be a cool modern garden for every bachelor, whether it's the city banker with his rooftop space for entertaining or the newly independent divorcee retiring into the city rather than out to the country and wanting a city garden to enjoy for gardening and relaxing in. So next time your London garden is looking a bit tired check out the garden of the single male living next door and get a few tips for a fab garden design.

APARTMENT PATIO AND DECK GARDENS

With a little care and consideration, you'll be able to have a garden on a deck or patio of an apartment. You can enjoy herb, flow or even veggie gardens from your apartment deck/patio. You really don't need much space to have a good garden. Here are some recommendations for how you can garden in a space no more than 8 sq ft. With a little planning in just minutes you can have a great garden. First you'll need some plant growing containers. You can find a variety of sizes to choose from but try to stick to 18 inch or smaller. You may also think about hanging some of your planting containers to give you additional space on your deck or patio. This is easily done by hanging hooks to attach the hangers to - but be sure to check with your apartment manager before drilling holes or making any big changes to your deck area.

As far as veggies go you will find a big variety to pick from. Some favorites include tomatoes of course, but also carrots, peppers, squash (think about growing these from a hanging basket) or radishes. The variety of flowers available for planting in a small garden such as deck gardens is virtually limitless. As for which herbs are best to grow - think about what you like to cook and use popular varieties that are easy to grow like basil, rosemary and thyme. But you don't have to limit your garden to just flowers, veggies and herbs - you can also consider alternative gardens like Feng Shui or Bonsai gardens. The basic concept of Feng Shui gardens is to arrange the plants in way so that there are no straight lines. These are great ways to show off small statues of Buddha or other Asian garden art.

Bonsai gardens are popular to set up both indoors and outdoors. Of course Bonsai are small trees that have been sculpted into appealing shapes. When thinking about what you want to plan a critical factor in choosing is thinking about how much sunlight your apartment deck gets. This can determine what you grow. Make sure the plants get plenty of sun. This can be an issue when setting up a patio or deck garden. The bottom line is that any sort of garden can be done in a small setting. After all, even though it's an apartment - it is still your home.

CATS, SHADE AND GRAVITY - A NATURAL PART OF YOUR GARDEN PATIO DESIGN

Those living in condos and apartments may love to have a beautiful garden of flowers. Sadly, no one knows of a flower garden design without dirt. This is not readily available if you live in shared dwellings.

You should know, there are managers of these condos and apartments that do not have a problem with a resident planting a garden if it is away from the area where people come and go to their apartments.

They could actually be benefiting from your plantings as long as the flower garden design is attractive looking. If you are not the container gardening type, you never know until you ask. They may say no and give you a look. Instead, they might tell you a good area for planting your garden.

We are going to suppose, for the purpose of writing this piece, that your only option is a patio garden. A patio garden design will require that you follow rules that are fairly strict, but they will allow you to have great looking flowers that will grow.

Before anything else, you will want to plan the patio garden design and eliminate the use of plants that will need full sun for longer than a small number of hours per day. One thing you may not consider is that part of the sky will not be visible due to the apartment building you are living in. The only way this will not be a problem is if your patio garden is on a roof top because you live on the top floor. But, most patios have a roof - even top ones - so this blocks the sky as well.

Next, potted plants are prime sleeping, eating and other unmentionable areas for cats. This is especially true before the plants have had a chance to grow and take up more of the soil. So this attracts cats to the soil to do their unmentionable acts. Beginning plants can be killed by cats napping on them in the sunshine, keeping them from growing, but cat urine can do just as much damage because it contains ammonia.

If there are not families of cats running all over your apartment complex, then you do not have to be concerned with this. However, many apartment complexes have to take action to protect their patio garden design. There are ways to discourage cats from getting in your plants. Using a fertilizer with chemicals can keep them away while feeding the plants.

Just like many other animals, cats are very particular about what will stop them from doing something they want to do.

Another method using skewers placed in the soil of the pot will help. Make sure they are placed in the pots while seeding so you will not run the risk of injuring root systems.

Buy plenty of skewers. The cat is quite unrelenting when they make up their mind they want to sleep in one spot. They may just curl up around the skewers if there are not many. These are usually found at your grocers and are not expensive. Wooden ones will do just fine. When the plant has had a chance to grow the soil is not as appealing and the skewers may be able to be taken out.

One thing to remember. If you water before taking off for the day, plants that you have purchased from your local growers that are healthy and mature should be checked to make certain your patio is not angled in a direction that keeps the water from draining from the pot. The need for modification may be necessary or you may need a particular type of pot for the flower garden design.

CHAPTER 7
SAVE MONEY & EAT HEALTHIER WITH AN EDIBLE GARDEN LANDSCAPE

Edible Garden Landscaping, also called front-yard gardening, edible landscaping, garden landscaping all refer to the same type of gardening practice, one that focuses on plants that provide food - fruits, vegetables, nuts, herbs, roots and so on. There are many benefits to an edible landscape including saving money on groceries and enjoying food that is fresher and more nutritious than the produce in our supermarkets which is often picked before it is ripe (nutrients aren't developed yet either) and shipped long distances.

IS EDIBLE LANDSCAPE GARDENING FOR YOU?

Do you want to grow food for your family to help reduce grocery expenses and help recession-proof your household budget? Then this type of gardening is a perfect way to help achieve that goal. Seeds cost next to nothing and in just a few weeks you'll be able to start enjoying the fresh greens or radishes that you've planted as a border planting. Other plants started from seed take longer, but they are well worth the wait!

Buying established nursery plants is also an option, and while it's more expensive than seeds, you'll be able to enjoy home-grown treats sooner than if you started from seed and the cost is still less than what you'd spend at the supermarket for the same items.

WHERE THERE'S A WILL, THERE'S A WAY

A large space is not required to grow fruits and vegetables, so don't let something like living in a city apartment hold you back. The key to achieving your goal of growing your own foods is to use the space you have as efficiently as possible. Even apartment dwellers can grow herbs, greens, tomatoes, and even specialized varieties of fruits. Many years ago, I lived in a courtyard-style apartment building in Chicago and was able to grow herbs and lettuce on my window sill! Container gardens are easy to establish and care for; all you need to do is decide how many containers you can accommodate, and provide water and light.

DOESN'T GROWING YOUR OWN FOOD TAKE A LOT OF TIME?

When you integrate fruits and vegetables into your landscape or a container garden, it doesn't take as much time as you'd think to take care of the plants, garden beds, etc. In fact, there's been many an evening after work that I end up wondering around the yard looking for something to do! This is partly because of the type of plants you'll be adding to your landscape. For example, an edible groundcover growing in a garden bed helps squeeze out weeds, thus eliminating the time you need to spend weeding. Utilize the practice of companion planting you'll also be able to control harmful pests naturally - yet another time saver. I also highly recommend using soaker hoses. You can water plants slowly at the roots where it's most beneficial and causes the least leaf damage, and you don't have to worry about timing the sprinklers, moving the hose, trampling plants and so forth.

Admittedly, when it's time to harvest the garden bounty, I spend more time in the yard and kitchen. But, when you're picking foods you've grown yourself, the extra time is rewarded by fresh delicious food that is not only good for you, but is helping to trim your grocery costs.

THE POSSIBILITIES ARE NEARLY LIMITLESS.

Think outside the garden plot. You don't have to have a dedicated vegetable garden to grow great tasting fruits and vegetables. Plant strawberries, nasturtiums, low-growing kitchen herbs, or a creeping berry as a ground cover. Train peas and pole beans to climb a trellis or arbor, or plant grapes vines as a perennial option. Add a fruit or nut tree or two for shade, and use berry bushes for shrubs or hedges. Even in neighborhoods that require perfectly manicured lawns and landscapes, edible plantings are a great option! They flower in the spring, produce attractive fruit and have attractive foliage in the fall. And, they can help reduce the amount of work you need to do to maintain the look of your yard. The bigger your landscape beds and more edible plants you have, the less lawn there is to care for!

GARDENING 101 - MAKING MONEY FROM YOUR HOME GARDEN

The concept of healthy and green living has motivated countless people to pursue gardening seriously which is why they are ever more interested in growing plants and trees. A garden has become a pivotal part of any landscape and it is used to accent the property or even to earn money from home. There are many people who are on a continuous lookout for lucrative options of making money from home.

More and more people these days are trying out gardening and landscaping commercially as it is very creative and interesting.

68

You do not necessarily require a big budget to try out your hands on making money from your garden. If you love gardening then you can turn your passion into a small home-based business that can help you financially. A home garden presents numerous options and it can open doors for you if you are willing to earn money from home.

EARNING PROFITS FROM YOUR GARDEN

If you happen to have a large area on your property then you can use it to set up a beautiful and profitable garden. A profitable garden is perfect for anyone who stays at home and wants to keep themselves busy and make money at the same time. There are many ways of yielding profits from your garden. You can deal in different varieties of plants and shrubs through a backyard nursery. However, if you do not have a budget or space for it; you can still go ahead and try out other interesting ways. Selling home-grown produce in the flea markets or other local markets is a great and inexpensive option. You can grow different types of aromatic herbs, fruits, berries and vegetables. Apart from these, you can also offer bulbs, flowering seeds and seedlings for sale.

GROW DELECTABLE FRUITS AND BERRIES

Fruits are very versatile and they can be consumed raw or can be used in several delicious recipes. Everyone loves them and some fruits like Strawberries, Apples, Peaches, Blackberries and Raspberries are extensively grown in home gardens. Apart from these fruits, you can also consider growing Paw Paw, Persimmon Tree, Walnuts, Gooseberries, Pears, etc. These fruits can be sold in the flea markets or other local markets in the town. Organically cultivated produce is very much in demand these days and people prefer to buy home-grown produce as it is fresh and healthy. By selling these fruits, you can earn money from your garden and on the other hand you can also save a lot by consuming home-grown fruits and veggies. Growing your edible plants will bring down your grocery bills.

GROW SEASONAL VEGETABLES AND HERBS

Seasonal vegetables like Spring Onion, Capsicum, Pepper, Cabbage, Celery, Tomato, Carrots, Beans, Squash, Cucumber, Garlic, etc are excellent for selling. Apart from these, you can offer good quality aromatic herbs like Marjoram, Sage, Thyme, Coriander, Basil, Oregano and Rosemary. Most of these herbs are not easily available but they are in great demand. Many people use these herbs in cooking and they require the freshest stock for their recipes.

OFFER SEEDS, BULBS AND SEEDLINGS

Seeds of flowering plants and native varieties are inexpensive and you can purchase them in bulk from a wholesale dealer. Bulbs of flowering plants like Daffodil, Lily, Gladiolus, Amaryllis, Allium, Caladium, Canna, Iris, Dahlia, etc. are also quite popular with home gardeners. You can offer all these varieties through your backyard garden to earn profits.

5 SIMILARITIES BETWEEN GARDENING AND YOGA

For last 3 years, I've moved to an apartment from camped apartment. After countless failed attempts of indoor gardening I decided to wait until I had my own apartment-today I can say with dare that I've my own yard to try gardening. One of the very first things that I did when I moved into the apartment was calling up my dad and asking for some flower bulbs to set up my own garden in the apartment. I don't have much knowledge about gardening. But I experience something pretty amazing and therapeutic in playing with the dirt. It's akin to the experience that I feel on my yoga mat.

Now you may definitely be wondering that why this crazy man is linking gardening with yoga, aren't you? So here are the five similarities that I found between yoga and gardening:

Require mindfulness. Studying the signs of lack or growth in plants requires mindfulness. Identifying how much light a plant needs and when is also a challenge that I'm still honing. Same is true for yoga too - it also requires mindfulness. You need to read your every breathe and movement in the body for doing yoga properly.

Finding connection. Seeing the plants grow and flowers bloom is a certainly energizing experience, especially when I know that I did something to make it happen. Thus, we find a connection between ourselves and growing of plants. In yoga too we learn that there is a connection between us and universe. So when I nourish something and help it in growing, I feel even more connected.

Removing any weeds. If you want a plant to grow, you've to ensure that the area surrounding that plant does not have any weeds. Otherwise other plants may absorb the nutrients from soil. Same is true for yoga too. In order to dedicate your mind to your yoga practice you must learn to stay away from distractions that pull your attention from the practice.

Looking for balance. A healthy and beautiful garden is the one that's filled with a variety of plants and has flowers of various colors. Too many plants of one type don't only spoil the aesthetic of garden but also affect the balance of nutrients in soil. And yoga is also about balance. A lot of active poses at the same time can be exhausting, while a whole lot of passive poses can become the cause of sluggishness in body. To get the desired results you must have a perfect balance of both.

Dirty work. You may not always be interested in making your hands dirty of soil, but the more time you invest the better your plants grow in the garden. And in yoga, it may seem hard to hold yourself in certain poses for as long as your teacher wants but the longer you hold the better you get on that particular pose (which ultimately results in health benefits).

HERB GARDEN TIPS

TIPS TO GROW A HERB GARDEN

Whether you are a serious gardener who wishes to grow a robust crop of herbs, or just grow a pleasant and aromatic garden, here are some things to help you along the way. Herbs are used for being used in salads to spicing up the flavor of your favorite dishes. In any event, herbs allow just a little snip to bring the flavor you desire. Even a small indoor garden can provide herbs for a small family on a consistent basis.

Using herbs fresh is delightful, however, many times if you have a large crop you will want properly dry them for preserving and using them later. First you must cut off the tops and wash them in cold water. Tying the stems together, hang them upside down in a paper bag and secure the stems at the opening with a tie. You will then want to hang them at an elevated location so as to allow nothing to be touching the drying herbs. In about 3 weeks you will be able to remove the bag and crumble the herbs to be dried further in the oven. You will want to set your oven at warm, nothing above 100 degrees. Leave your herbs in the oven just long enough to ensure they are thoroughly dried. Now all you do is store them in an air tight container!

TYPICAL HERBS GROWN

BASIL

Basil is a very colorful herb with pink blossoms and is sometimes used purely for it's asthetics in a garden. Basil takes about 7-10 days to start to grow and will grow about 1 1/2 feet. Because they grow so tall, it is best to put about a foot in between plants. This herb is great for use with tomato dishes.

CHIVES

This herb is grown from small bulbs or can also be grown by seed as well. The growth of the chive looks a bit like grass growing. While it does get about a foot tall, you can space these closer together than basil at about 1/2 foot. These are solid growers even in colder climates. This herb as well as being tasty is also pretty with flowering. This herb can be used in just about every salad or sauce around.

DILL

This herb is an almost feathery plant. It has little yellow flowers and can grow to be about 2 to 2 1/2 feet tall. These plants are not really good with trying to transplant though but you can space them pretty close together - about 4 inches apart. While this is a good salad addition, this is many times used for pickling vegetables.

MARJORAM

This herb grows great in all climates. Grows about a foot tall and you can space them about 1/2 foot apart. This is a great herb for fish and soups.

MINT

Mint is very thick in it's growth so you need to space these plants about a foot apart up to about 2 feet high. While commonly enjoyed in many beverages of choice, this is also a great addition to a salad or lamb dish.

SAGE

This is a pretty herb with blue sprouts of flowers. They grow pretty high so space your plants about a foot apart. This is great to flavor a good dressing or some of your white meat choices.

THYME

This herb mimics a little bush in it's growth. You need to cut the leaves before the blossoms open if you are going to dry. Gets to be about a foot tall so space plants anywhere from 6-10 inches apart. This is a great herb for soups or gravy.

So here were a few that make cooking so much more flavorful. Once you get a solid garden with these herbs......dare to experiment! Have fun getting more flavorful way in a pretty and much more cost effective manner.

GARDEN FURNITURE: THE SUITABILITY FACTOR

The mankind of the present world wants peace due to enormous stress because of the work load at the work place. Gardens are the places where the person can get peace if he is really interested to achieve it. These provide the person not only peace but also the tranquility. When you go to your indoor garden that is attached to your home, your mood and life is totally transformed. You want to relax and for this you need garden furniture in your beautiful garden.

When you sit on this beautiful piece made of wood, you will undergo complete rejuvenation of the body, mind as well as soul. Apart from this, it also enhances the beauty of the garden. The principle elements of composition of this type of furniture are wood, cane or plastic. In the category of wood, the teak offers the high level of resistance against the natural disasters.

LUXURY GARDEN FURNITURE: THE OPTIONS OF CHOICE

If you love wooden garden furniture and want to install it in your garden, you can select the material. If you invest the money in the teak furniture, it is a very healthy option because it adds to the perfection and sophistication of your garden. If you spend the extra bucks for this type of purchase, do not get worried at all because it is a long term investment.

There is high amount of durability that is offered by this type of furniture. The teak furniture does contain the essential oils that offer it resistance against the wear and tear and besides this such wood is highly durable.

LIGHT WEIGHT GARDEN FURNITURE:

If you want the light weight garden furniture, the material you need to opt for is the cane. Apart from this, it is also used for the manufacturing of benches, chairs as well as tables not generally meant for the purpose of garden. It is very good as far as the cleaning is concerned. You can easily take this furniture from one place to another keeping in mind its light weight.

RATAN GARDEN FURNITURE:

Many people use the rattan garden furniture in the present times. It also acts as classic furniture and is used in both the gardens s well as the lawns. It offers you the resistance to all the type of weather conditions.

PLASTIC GARDEN FURNITURE:

If you rally do not have much money in the pocket and want something truly cheap and strong, you can go for the plastic garden furniture. Such pieces come in different colors like green, blue as well as pink. Apart from this, you can also purchase aluminum or wrought iron furniture.

CONCLUSION
THE PRACTICE OF GARDENING FOR KIDS

If you are a nature lover, then the practice of gardening certainly brings you a step closer to nature. Gardening is a part of horticulture that allows you to grow plants of your choice. You can also create a lively green and soothing area near your house by sowing seeds. The art of gardening needs proper care and practice, and a result gives you colorful flowers, fruits and vegetables. All you require to start gardening is a certain space. If you have a front or back yard, you can easily start working on your gardening activities. Selecting the right space or area plays a pivotal role in the process of gardening. However, people living in multi-storied apartments hardly find any gardening space. In such cases, they can take the initiative on an apartment portico, terrace or roofs.

While sowing seeds or cultivating plants on the soil, make sure the plants get sufficient sunlight so that they can grow. In addition to sufficient sunlight, make sure the soil has an abundance of nutrients and minerals. Soil nutrients are very crucial, especially if you plan to cultivate edible parts like grapes, cucumbers, tomatoes etc. These support your plants while growing.

Other than sunlight and productive soil, you also need to keep in mind that your plants need to get sufficient water to grow and remain healthy. Water for a sturdy plant is as important as the requirement of oxygen for our subsistence. The practice of gardening begins during childhood and helps the kids aware of the significance of nature and gardening in their lives. However, one of the most challenging things for the kid is to keep the soil perfectly soggy. To keep the plants alive, water is required, but kids should be careful that they do not give too much of it. The best thing to do in such cases is to touch the soil with your hand. If you touch it and it is dry, then it probably needs a greater amount of water. If it is already moist and softer, you can wait awhile before adding more water.

Kids who are doing it for the first time should know that you can place the plants into the soil either directly or through a vessel or container. You will find most of the garden containers used in urban gardening are made of crates, empty cartons or stacks of tires. It is always crucial for you to choose the right plants before you start digging in the yard. This is because; some plants grow better in their natural surroundings. Such plants are referred to as native species and are considered as the perfect plant for those who have just started their gardening plans. They grow better with the usual amounts of sunlight and water in their areas. On the other hand, for cultivating non-native species, kids must be acquainted with all the basics about those plants. This includes, finding out the required amounts of water, sunlight and the nourishment needed for growing these plants. In addition, you also need to know which types of soil suit those non-native species best.

One thing that you must set in your mind while gardening is that you should never get bored. Gardening all together includes a lot of fun, challenges experiences for kids. Those who have never tried gardening before thing initially that it sounds quite challenging for them. However, if you spend a good time in learning what gardening is, you will surely create a pleasant and refreshing environment around you.

Made in the USA
Columbia, SC
05 December 2021

50509496R00046